MOVING PAST THE HURT

RECLAIMING YOUR IDENTITY IN CHRIST

CHERYL DYSON-BENNETT

MOVING PAST THE HURT
RECLAIMING YOUR IDENTITY IN CHRIST

© 2024 Cheryl Dyson-Bennett
All rights reserved. This book is printed in the United States of America. No part of This book may be used or reproduced in any form or by any means -electronic, mechanical, photocopy, recording, or otherwise - without written permission of the publisher, except in the case of brief quotations embodied in critical articles or reviews.

THE HOLY BIBLE, NEW INTERNATIONAL VERSION, NIV
Copyright© 1973, 1978, 1984, 2011, by Biblica, Inc. Used by permission. All rights reserved worldwide.

Scriptures taken from the New King James Version. Copyright© 1982 by Thomas Nelson. Used by permission. All rights reserved. Scripture quotations marked KJV are from the King James Version of the Bible.

Scripture quotations marked NLT are from the Holy Bible, New Living Translation, Copyright© 1996, 2004, 2007. Used by permission. All rights reserved.

Scripture quotations marked The Message are from The Message: The Bible in Contemporary English, Copyright© 1993, 1994, 1995, 2000, 2001, 2002. Used by permission. All rights reserved.

Designed for Greatness, LLC
Atlanta, Georgia
www.designed4greatness.com

You are Designed for Greatness; I am Designed for Greatness;
We are Designed for Greatness

CONTENTS

Introduction v

Chapter 1: Strength From Above 1
The Story of My Pain, Struggles, and God's Unwavering Mercy

Chapter 2: Finding Solace in God 5

Chapter 3: Looking Into God's Mirror 13
Seeing Yourself as God Sees You

Chapter 4: Mending 21
Finding Total Healing from God

Chapter 5: Confronting the Beast 27
Dealing with Fear and Anxiety

Chapter 6: Baggage 35
Dealing with the Memories of the Past

Chapter 7: Looking Into God's Mirror II 43
Mind Reconfiguration

Chapter 8: Newness 51
Deciding to Live Again

Chapter 9: Rubies 61
You Are More Than What You Think

Chapter 10: Becoming a Burden Bearer 67

Chapter 11: Being in the Company of the Strong . . . 77
Finding the Right Environment

Chapter 12: Where Do I Go From Here? 83
Your Journey to a New Beginning

Conclusion 91
Afterword 93
About the Author 95
Cheryl Dyson-Bennett's Publications 97

INTRODUCTION

Hurt is something every one of us has an idea of in varying degrees. It's part of the human existence. There is really no one on earth that has not experienced some measure of hurt from betrayal by trusted people, loss of loved ones, divorce trauma, heartbreak, and other types of hurt. It's practically impossible to avoid hurt throughout one's lifetime. The inevitability that we will experience hurt is not the issue, the core of the matter is our response in that period of hurt. How do we handle hurt while we are hurting? This and some variants of it are frequently asked questions by people going through a season of hurt.

Some people that have been hurt sometimes feel the need to retaliate. They feel they have a score to settle. Retaliation has never helped anyone to move past hurt, it can only complicate matters. Some on the other hand internalize hurt to avoid confrontation with the people that hurt them. This is also not an effective method of healing. Hurt suppressed or internalized often leads to depression or bitterness towards the one that caused the hurt.

The most appropriate means of healing and moving past hurt is to let God handle the matter on your behalf. Jesus is our advocate; we must let Him plead our case. The word of God teaches us that if it is possible on your part, live at peace with everyone. Do not avenge yourselves but leave room for God's wrath. For it is written: "Vengeance is Mine; I will repay, says the Lord." **Romans 12:19 NIV** On the contrary, "If your enemy is hungry, feed Him; if he is thirsty, give Him a drink. For in so doing, you will heap burning coals on His head." **Romans 12:20 NIV**

I concede that allowing God to avenge us can be extremely hard because it's totally the opposite of what we are familiar with or what our flesh wants. The reason this is difficult is because it requires forgiving those that hurt you and that's the last thing anyone hurting wants to do.

This is the most effective way to win. Winning with God requires you not to throw a single punch but to surrender all things to Him. Surrendering to God means to let go of the hurt and allow Him to deal with the issues however he sees fit. You won't be able to do this if you don't have an absolute confidence in the compassion of God towards you and His ability to right every wrong.

Surrendering to God starts with putting your confidence in Him and not in yourself or in another person for that matter. It means judging God faithful enough to get justice for you.

"For I the Lord love justice; I hate robbery and wrong; I will faithfully give them their recompense." **Isaiah 61:8 ESV**

You can count on God to get you the justice you deserve, He won't let you down. There is no one that has ever called on God's name and regretted it. God is faithful.

"For there is no difference between the Jew and the Greek: for the same Lord over all is rich unto all that call upon Him. For whosoever shall call upon the name of the Lord shall be saved". -**Romans 10.12 -13 KJV**

Surrendering to God will require you to follow His principles and ways of doing things. You can't fight back when someone or some people hurt you because "the wrath of man worketh not the righteousness of God" - **James 1:20 KJV**

God will not bend His principles for anyone, when we surrender to Him, we must let go of everything and take on His yoke to learn His methods of doing things. It is in doing this that we find total healing and peace of mind.

God's method of healing starts with total forgiveness of those that hurt you. God's system of forgiveness requires us not to take offense in any wrong done to us but to forgive the person in advance.

"Then came Peter to Him, and said, Lord, how oft shall my brother sin against me, and I forgive Him? till seven times? Jesus saith unto Him, I say not unto thee, Until seven times: but, Until seventy times seven". -**Matthew 18:21 – 22 KJV**

Instead of striving to deal with hurt by yourself or trying to get back at those that hurt you, it is wise to look to God for total healing. We always create a bigger mess trying to do things in our own way, the flesh doesn't bring any profit. You may appear foolish by others for leaving it all in God's hand to get justice for you, but it won't be the first time that God will be using seemingly foolish methods to work out great things.

"..the foolishness of God is wiser than men; and the weakness of God is stronger than men". – **1 Corinthians 1:25 ESV**

It requires absolute faith in God to follow His methods because there are times it may not look reasonable to the human brain, but the human brain in itself is limited in understanding.

There is healing in God. There is justice in Him. Quit trying to do things by yourself, it will lead you to the middle of nowhere.

When you put your confidence in God and surrender all to Him to do it His way, the Lord goes to work to ensure that you're not put to shame. He ensures you get justice; He heals you of all hurt and its accompanying pain.

"... I am the LORD that healeth thee". **Exodus 15:26 KJV**

This book was written to encourage and motivate readers to trust in Jesus. In your own personal experiences of pain and struggle, it is my hope that you will be empowered to put your faith and trust in Jesus for all your needs. Through trusting in Jesus, I have found solace and serenity in difficult times. It is my desire that readers can also draw on Jesus's strength and courage to help them through their own trials.

When we put our trust in Jesus, he never disappoints us. He is always there to help us out of whatever situation we find ourselves in. Through this book, it is my goal that readers will be inspired to put their faith in Jesus and find complete healing and peace. In turn, they will be able to share this with others and help them to find their own healing and solace in Jesus.

"In the midst of life's tumultuous storms, there exists an unwavering sanctuary within us, a beacon of resilience and unyielding strength that emanates even in the darkest moments. The story of perseverance amid trials, the narrative of enduring faith, echoes the profound truth that adversity is not the end but a transformative passage towards personal growth."

STRENGTH FROM ABOVE

THE STORY OF MY PAIN, STRUGGLES, AND GOD'S UNWAVERING MERCY

When it comes to understanding pain, words can never quite capture the intensity and depth of it. All individuals experience pain differently and words just cannot do justice to the magnitude of its power. It is only when we have gone through the same hurt that we can truly understand how another person is feeling.

I have had my own share of pain and hurt, and I have also seen the mercy and grace of God. I have seen how he has been able to bring healing and solace to a heart that is deeply wounded. So, I know how you feel, and I want to remind you that His love will be enough to get you through this. No matter what you are going through, God will always be there to catch you when you fall.

The capacity to truly understand and empathize with someone's pain is not just about being able to interpret the words they express. It goes much deeper, requiring us to fully immerse ourselves into the emotions they are experiencing. Having walked my own path of agony and hurt, I have come to truly recognize the profound and complex nature of these sentiments. Despite the immense suffering I have endured, I have also been a firsthand witness to the power of mercy and divine assistance from God, which has been a healing force in my deeply scarred heart.

As I reflect on my own journey, I am reminded of the importance of being present for others in their times of need. It is not enough to simply offer words of comfort or advice; true empathy requires us to fully embrace the pain and emotions of those around us. It is through this deep understanding and connection that we can offer genuine support and healing.

In my own experience, it was the unwavering love and compassion from those around me that helped me find my way through the darkest moments of my life. And now, having emerged stronger and more resilient, I am committed to being a source of support and comfort for others who are struggling. For it is through our shared experiences of pain and healing that we can truly connect and uplift one another.

In the midst of life's tumultuous storms, there exists an unwavering sanctuary within us, a beacon of resilience and unyielding strength that emanates even in the darkest moments. The story of perseverance amid trials, the narrative of enduring faith, echoes the profound truth that adversity is not the end but a transformative passage towards personal growth.

In the story of one's pain, struggle, and the enduring grace of divinity, lies an invaluable lesson, a testament to the unyielding spirit dwelling within each of us. It's a reminder that while life's trials may appear insurmountable, they are but chapters in a larger narrative, a story of triumph over tribulations.

It beckons us to embrace resilience, to stand steadfast in the face of uncertainty, and to seek solace in our unwavering faith. For within the depths of despair lies the seed of unwavering hope, an anchor that steadies us through life's tempests.

This chronicle teaches us the art of fortitude to persist despite adversity, to endure amidst chaos, and to emerge stronger, wiser, and more resolute. It implores us to harness the power of faith, not merely as a refuge but as a catalyst for transformative change, a force that propels us forward when the path seems obscured.

Amidst the complexities of relationships, the unpredictability of circumstances, and the trials that test our very being, this narrative serves as a testament to the indomitable human spirit. It calls upon each soul to recognize their intrinsic resilience, to draw strength from within, and to forge ahead on the path of unwavering determination.

May this book inspire you to embrace your own journey to navigate the storms with unwavering courage, to find solace in unwavering faith, and to emerge from the darkest of nights, illuminated by the light of resilience and enduring hope.

It's about-facing trials with unwavering courage, finding resilience in the face of adversity, and holding onto faith despite the storms. This narrative is a testament to enduring challenges, summoning strength from within, and discovering the power to rise above life's harshest moments. It's an account that unveils the rawness of human struggles, the unwavering spirit to persevere, and the profound impact of unwavering faith. This journey speaks volumes about resilience, hope, and the indomitable human spirit.

"Confidence in God gives us strength and courage to face the challenges that come our way. It allows us to have a sense of peace, no matter what we are going through. It gives us hope and joy in the midst of trials and tribulations. It gives us the assurance that no matter what happens, God loves us, and he will never leave us."

FINDING SOLACE IN GOD

I can assure you that there is hope in God even for a shattered heart. While people may judge you, misunderstand you, or even criticize you for the pain they caused, you can always reach out to God. He is close to the brokenhearted and saves those who are crushed in spirit. You will always find peace and solace in Him. There are times that your immediate environment may seem hostile. Sometimes, you may even have to escape from your thoughts. You must learn to reach out for God's hand for solace and comfort. Here is what God says;

"So do not fear, for I am with you; do not be dismayed, for I am your God. I will strengthen you and help you; I will uphold you with my righteous right hand". - **Isaiah 41:10 NIV**

This is God's promise to you. He never goes back on His word, all you need to do is to quit attempting to do things your way, surrender all to Him and let Him help you out. God is for you; he is always on your side. He will fight for you; he will wipe away your tears and comfort you on every side.

There are people that multiply their pain by seeking comfort in people that further intensify their problems. Some confided in individuals that later took advantage of their vulnerability and created a bigger mess for them.

Humans generally have a threshold of what they can stand. Some genuine people may later get wearied when you keep reaching out to them for comfort. The good news is that God has no threshold. You will never wear Him out. He will never get tired of you. He will not condemn you for your mistakes and weaknesses, he is infinite in mercy.

"Therefore, the Lord waits to be gracious to you; therefore, he will rise up to show mercy to you. For the Lord is a God of justice; blessed are all those who wait for Him." - **Isaiah 30:18** NRS

Seeking Solace in God

Finding solace in God means throwing your issues into His capable hands, letting go of hurts, pains, and betrayal in exchange for His comfort.

When people find themselves in some not so good situations, they tend to seek solace in things as a coping mechanism. Some turn to drugs, some find solace in parties, many others turn to other things which don't really bring any lasting solution. Some resort to talking with certain individuals who later get wearied of them. A lasting and effective solution is obtainable in God. The beautiful thing is that God wants to help you in your down moment only if you will reach out to Him.

You don't need to seek solace in another thing aside God. He understands your situation. God will not grow weary of you.

Confidence in God

God's faithfulness is not just found in the fact that he always keeps His word, but it is also found in the fact that he is powerful enough to do anything. He is able to bring about a solution to even the most difficult problems. He is able to take the worst circumstances and bring about something good and beautiful. His strength and ability are not limited, and he is able to do more than we could ever ask or imagine.

No matter how deep the issues are that we face, we can trust that God is able to bring light into our darkness and bring peace into our chaos. He is able to take brokenness and turn it into something good. We can trust that His power and strength is greater than anything that we ever encounter. He will never let us down and will always be there to help us in our time of need.

When one is confident in God, it is not just a feeling but a lifestyle. It is an assurance that God will take care of us and provide for us, even when times are tough. It is an understanding that God will not abandon us, even if he allows us to go through struggles and hardships. It is an acceptance that God will use our struggles and hardships to refine us and make us stronger. It is a belief that God will never leave us, no matter what.

Confidence in God means having faith in His plan for us. It is trusting that His plan is the best for us and that he will work it out for our own good. It is trusting in His promises, even when it seems like he is not answering our prayers. It is believed that God will use the circumstances of our lives to bring about good for us. It is having a heart of gratitude for what he has done and will continue to do in our lives.

Confidence in God gives us strength and courage to face the challenges that come our way. It allows us to have a sense of peace, no matter what we are going through. It gives us hope and joy in the midst of trials and tribulations. It gives us the assurance that no matter what happens, God loves us, and he will never leave us.

Love Beckons You

The closest thing to God's love for you is the genuine love of a caring mother for her infant child. It's the closest we can think of yet, there is still a wide gap between it and God's love.

God, in attempting to describe His love, asks if a mother can forget her nursing child. He said, though a mother can forget her suckling child, yet he will not forget you.

"Can a woman forget her sucking child, that she should not have compassion on the son of her womb? Yea, they may forget, yet will I not forget thee. Behold, I have graven thee upon the palms of my hands..." **Isaiah 49:15 -16 KJV**

I struggled with this idea that a woman can forget her nursing child until one day I saw a woman that just gave birth lying helpless beside her baby. She was in serious pain, so intense that she couldn't breastfeed the baby. Then, I realized the point God was making. There are times when the mother herself will be in a difficult situation, a situation that may prevent her from being able to care for the child. God is never going to be in this situation. He doesn't have a personal problem. And he cares for you with perfect care. Why don't you throw yourself in His hand and allow Him to take care of you?

If you have ever lost a loved one or suffered some other deep pain and hurt, you will realize clearly that there are some levels of pain that only the comfort from God and of God can soothe.

There is a pain that can penetrate the soul. Pain so deep, no words can heal. There are hurts that cannot be explained with words, this is where one must reach out for the comfort of God.

The thing with God's comfort is that it is administered to us on a personal basis. That is, comfort is designed specifically to take care of your pain. It comes to you in a personal way so that it addresses everything involved in the pain. Only God can do such a thing.

Living life is tough. You face endless challenges, some of which are so painful, that you cannot handle them a second time. Trying to cope with the agony that surpasses your limit is a battle in itself. It takes immense strength and resilience to keep going in the face of such pain. But how do you cope? What methods can you adopt to deal with the overwhelming emotions that come with certain wounds?

Sometimes, the wounds that cut the deepest are the ones that only you can truly understand. The pain can be so profound that others may struggle to empathize with you. It may even seem like you are exaggerating the extent of your suffering. However, in reality, you may be downplaying it. You are the only one who knows the full extent of your pain and how it affects you. It is a lonely and excruciating experience, one that can leave you feeling isolated and misunderstood.

But you are not alone. Only God can fix such pain. It's His area of expertise. The wise thing is to pour your pain and hurt on God and allow Him to comfort you.

"Humble yourselves therefore under the mighty hand of God, that he may exalt you in due time: Casting all your care upon Him; for He careth for you". - **Peter 5:6 -7 ESV**

The beautiful thing about God's love and comfort is that it comes at no cost. God doesn't run an analysis of your mistakes nor judge your choices before he attends to you. He meets your needs out of His infinite love.

Drawing Strength from God

When people give up and quit after a long episode of negative experiences, it is usually not because they willingly want to give up, they quit because they lack the fortitude to keep holding on.

There are huge crisis that if prolonged have the capacity to overwhelm the best of us, we find help by drawing strength from God.

Isaiah 40:29 - 32: KJV

"He giveth power to the faint; and to them that have no might he increaseth strength. Even the youths shall faint and be weary, and the young men shall utterly fall: But they that wait upon the LORD shall renew their strength; they shall mount up with wings as eagles; they shall run, and not be weary; and they shall walk, and not faint."

In the midst of the pain, you are going through, you shouldn't allow it to overwhelm you before turning to God for reinforcement.

Learning How to Talk to God

There are people you talk to that drain the little energy you are trying to preserve. Have you seen people like that before? Talking to them literally drains you of all your energy.

Talking to God is directly the opposite of that. When you talk to God you are refilling your energy tank.

Prayer is a structure of exchange, exchange between you and God. You pour out your pain and hurt to Him and in exchange to get strength from Him, enough strength to properly handle the issue that was seemingly overwhelming.

"Hast thou not known? hast thou not heard that the everlasting God, the LORD, the Creator of the ends of the earth, fainteth not, neither is weary? There is no searching for His understanding. He giveth power to the faint; and to them that have no might he increaseth strength. Even the youths shall faint and be weary, and the young men shall utterly fall: But they that wait upon the LORD shall renew their strength; they shall mount up with wings as eagles; they shall run, and not be weary; and they shall walk, and not faint." -**Isaiah 40: 28 -31 KJV**

Talking to God in prayer doesn't have to be technical, you just pour out your heart to Him genuinely. The beautiful thing about communicating with God is that you can discuss any matter with Him.

There are religious people that think God is only interested in them going to heaven and doesn't bother about their affairs on earth. Of course, God is interested. He wants you to be fine through all your endeavors.

"…regardless of the circumstances surrounding your life currently, you are God's masterpiece. You were created for something extremely significant. God has a specific plan and purpose for your life."

LOOKING INTO GOD'S MIRROR

SEEING YOURSELF AS GOD SEES YOU

"I will praise thee; for I am fearfully and wonderfully made marvelous are thy works; and that my soul knoweth right well" -**Psalms 139 :14 KJV**

One of the prominent effects of hurt and pain is its subtle ability to change one's perception about oneself, and overall view of life. When people stay too long in the mud of hurt, usually, they start seeing themselves less than the way God sees them. They tend to think little of themselves and expect little out of life. They somehow allow the hurt to reshape their thinking, they view themselves and others from that lens of hurt.

Negative experiences can remold the image you have about yourself if you allow it. For instance, if you have suffered heartbreak or betrayal from a person, you absolutely relied on, you start thinking something is wrong with you. You may entertain the thought that perhaps you are not good enough.

Allowing this sort of thought to linger will greatly affect your image. At this point, many people start doing ridiculous and demeaning things just to gain acceptance and validation.

This is negative conditioning and the only suitable antidote to it is to start seeing yourself the way God sees you.

There is no one that has an accurate picture of who you truly are other than God, the one that created you. Unlike what you may currently believe about your life, God didn't create trash, he created a treasure. He didn't create an ugly piece of anything, you were beautifully and wonderfully made. Your past mistakes may make you seem imprudent, but you are not. God created you with the potential to make rational choices.

You must look beyond the hurt and pain and see God's intention for bringing you on earth. God does not make junk, he makes masterpieces. And you, regardless of the circumstances surrounding your life currently, you are His masterpiece. You were created for something extremely significant. God has a specific plan and purpose for your life.

Made in the Image of God

The law of nature shows that everything reproduces after its kind. Humans reproduce humans, animals give birth to other animals. You won't find coconuts on a Mango tree. Everything is of its own kind.

You were created in the image of God. That's a huge thing to take pride in. Being made in the image of God means you share similarities with God.

God is full of glory; you are a glorious being. Contrary to what circumstances might have made you to believe, you are valuable. You should be radiating glory because that's your nature.

Ignorance about your origin is what makes you think less of yourself. Imagine a lion cub thinking he is a rat because of some unpleasant circumstances. You must separate the incident from the person. Incidences are just events; they do not dictate who you are. Who you are is a function of your origin. That is the only accurate estimation of who you are. You originated from God. You were made in His image. Christ died for you. You see, you can only redeem a thing with something that has equivalent value. When God thought of redeeming you, Christ had to shed His blood.

"For scarcely for a righteous man will one die yet peradventure for a good man some would even dare to die. But God commendeth His love toward us, in that, while we were yet sinners, Christ died for us". - **Romans 5:7 – 8 KJV.**

The Force of Joy

When a person's esteem or image has been distorted owing to certain negative experiences, what follows most times is for that person to now hold a pessimistic view about their endeavors and life in general.

Aside from the fact that you will attract to your life what you consistently think of, it is also incredibly difficult for a person that holds a pessimistic view about things to attempt to carry out anything great or meaningful. Maintaining such a negative posture means settling for a life of mediocrity and unfulfillment. This is definitely not what any right-thinking person should settle for. But, hurt and pain rarely make people think right.

The Joy Therapy

"To appoint unto them that mourn in Zion, to give unto them beauty for ashes, the oil of joy for mourning, the garment of praise for the spirit of heaviness; that they might be called trees of righteousness, the planting of the LORD, that he might be glorified". -**Isaiah 61: 3 KJV**

The appropriate way to deal with sadness and a pessimistic mindset occasioned by past hurt and pain is to engage in the joy therapy. The joy therapy means to deliberately choose to be joyful at all times regardless of how you feel.

One major sign of strength is the ability to subdue your emotions and do what is right no matter how you feel. This is an incredible power that we all possess. A person who allows their emotions to dictate their lives will be a victim of so many forms of manipulation by people who will use their emotions against them.

One way to start taking charge of your emotions is to choose to be joyful in all situations. I must confess that this won't be an easy task in the beginning because there are times you won't feel like it. Sometimes you won't see the need or the reason to be joyful.

You see, in all our lives as humans, we have expressed happiness and excitement based on something tangible that we are pleased about. If someone gifted you a car, you are excited. You got a new job, you are delighted. You put on a nice dress, and someone gave you a compliment, you felt so nice about it. It has always been like that; you respond to something external that gives you something to be delighted about.

Meanwhile, the joy therapy works a little different from that. Here, you choose to be happy and joyful regardless of the situation or circumstance. Whether you see something exciting or not, you maintain your joy. Whether you get a good compliment when you dress your best or no one even notices you throughout the day, you still maintain your joy. Your joy level is not dependent on anything external, it is absolutely a resolution you decide to hold and hold firmly.

The thing about being resolute about your joy therapy is that it shields you from things that can further hurt you or cause some form of damage. You may not be able to control those that choose to hurt you, or control hurt itself, but what you can control is your response to it.

A lady was jilted by her lover of many years, a week later she saw pictures of Him and another lady on the internet having fun. She couldn't handle it and started contemplating suicide. I know that may sound extreme, but you cannot underestimate the power of depression. It is extremely dangerous. Joy helps to fight off depression.

How to Cultivate Joy

Since joy is not based on something external, that is, it is not dependent on anything; whether good or bad; it has to be sustained by something else for it to be effective.

What sustains joy is the awareness of the beautiful and secured plans that God has for you.

Here is what God says.

"I know what I'm doing. I have it all planned out—plans to take care of you, not abandon you, plans to give you the future you hope for". (**Jeremiah 29:11, The Message Bible**).

This kind of assurance from God in whom there is no

variableness; the one that never goes back on His word is the bedrock of a sustainable life of absolute joy.

The exciting thing about knowing the plans of God is that the beautiful plans that God has for you doesn't depend on what anyone did to you. The hurt, the pain, and the betrayal can't hinder or mitigate it. As a matter of fact, God in His wisdom uses the things that people did to hurt you to your advantage. He uses them as raw materials to produce something great for you. Here is why the Bible assures you that all things are going to work for your good. Not just the nice things but all things. Including the bad and ugly, because God has got your back, he finds a way to use those negative experiences for your good.

Being aware and having this conviction is what inspires joy and also preserves it.

Bank of Goodness

Since low self-esteem and distorted image of oneself can be traced to bankruptcy of the right thoughts, it is important to begin to reinforce the right thoughts into your mindset.

This requires consistent reading and storing up the word of God into your consciousness until you have a bank full of the right words. These words, if consistently engaged, will begin to have an effect on your thought life.

Your thoughts, which dictate your actions, will start following the pattern of the words you have stored up in your consciousness. After a while, the distorted view becomes corrected.

Have you ever been prescribed glasses to correct your eyes? A person with an eye problem, in effect, is close to a blind person though not blind. Depending on the problem, some people can't see something close to them, while some others can't see something far from them. When such a person goes to see the doctor, the result may be a prescription for glasses. Sometimes the purpose of the glasses is to correct the person's vision. The glasses work to correct the vision by allowing your eyes to focus light on the right spot on the retina. After a while, the distorted view is eradicated, and the person can now see accurately.

"The entrance of thy words giveth light; it giveth understanding unto the simple". -**Psalms 119:130 KJV**

Storing up God's word that addresses your situation is recommended to help you correct your distorted view about yourself by giving you abundant illumination until you see your accurate picture in Christ.

Like the glasses, the word helps you to fix your mind and your total consciousness on what God says about you. You now see yourself accurately. Instead of seeing a rejected person, you see a person totally loved by a caring father. Rather than seeing a worthless person, you begin to see a personality with an inestimable value.

All the distortions that affected your view through hurt, rejection, loss, betrayal and pain begin to give way. As you start thinking and seeing yourself the right way, your life starts accommodating the right things and the right people.

"God specializes in healing the brokenhearted but His offer to help must be accepted by you. Accepting His help entails you forgiving whoever hurt you, letting go of the hurt, and submitting to Him."

MENDING
FINDING TOTAL HEALING FROM GOD

Healing is a recovery from hurt or injury. When a person has gone through pain or hurt, healing is required for recovery. Recovery doesn't essentially mean the person won't remember the hurt; it just means that there won't be any commensurate pain attached to the memory. You must have experienced pain or sickness before healing can take place. While you were in pain, it may have seemed as if the pain would never end, however when you were treated by a doctor, it all went away. Even when you remember that episode, the memory didn't come with the pain you previously experienced, because it was all gone. You need to understand that getting healed from your past is very important because you can't get past the hurt unless you've been healed.

God specializes in healing the hurt and brokenhearted. He wants to heal you; He doesn't want you to continue living in pain. He loves you that much. He's always looking out for you;

He wants the best for you. The best thing you need right now is healing and He's more than willing to give it to you. Quit feeling sorry for yourself and come to Him for healing. He's the only one that can make all the pain go away. There is a common misconception people have about God. They believe God only cares about spiritual stuff but, He also cares about your emotional and mental health as well. They all matter to Him. He wants you to be healed from all the pain and hurt. He knows that you can only live a successful and happy life when all those are settled, you should know that too.

To experience total healing from pain and hurt you must be ready and willing to do these things:

1. Acknowledge God's Love

The love God has for us cannot be fathomed. He loves us beyond our imagination. His love has no limit and cannot be quantified. As a result of His love, he doesn't want us in pain. He wants us to live a life of peace and joy. God's love is unconditional and endless. He loves us regardless of what we've been through. Having people you love makes it easier to understand. Has anyone you love ever been in pain and you tried all you could do to ease their pain? Despite the fact that you're not omnipotent, you still did what you could. Now, you get a glimpse of what God feels when we are in pain. When you understand the love he has for you, you know he has got your back. You then rest in His abilities to ease your pain.

2. Come to God Just the Way You Are

Come without hiding anything.

God is merciful and loving, He cares so much about you. He doesn't care about your past or present, all he wants is to make you enjoy happiness and peace of mind. He doesn't discriminate, He loves you unconditionally. That is why he said in **Matthew 11:28 AMPC** - "Come to Me, all you who labor and are heavy-laden and overburdened, and I will cause you to rest. I will ease, relieve and refresh your souls." You should come to God with the pain and hurt. You don't hide in the presence of God; you bare all the hurt before Him. You present everything to Him and ask for His help.

When a patient comes to a doctor for diagnosis and treatment, he does not hide anything from him, he tells hm everything - the way he is feeling, the symptoms and full information. That's the way you ought to come to God - with everything.

Approach God without fear. He wants us to come to Him as we would come to a loving father - without fear. Have you ever been afraid to ask somebody for help and you later got to know that the person was open to it all along, you probably found this out when it was too late for you to benefit from it. Being able to come to God with boldness puts the enemy to shame. The enemy knows that coming to God without fear is the first step to total healing. The scriptures even stated that we should come boldly to God in order to get help in time of need. You should not be afraid of the person that wants to help you. He holds the solution to your problem, come to Him without fear.

"For we do not have a high priest who is unable to empathize with our weakness... Let us then approach God's throne of grace with confidence, so that we may receive mercy and find grace to help us in our time of need." - **Hebrews 4:15-16 NIV**

3. Accept His Help

God specializes in healing the brokenhearted but His offer to help must be accepted by you. Accepting His help entails you forgiving whoever hurt you, letting go of the hurt and submitting to Him.

Forgiving Whoever Hurt You

You cannot recover from hurt if you've not forgiven the person that hurt you. The interesting thing about not forgiving others is that the offender has since moved on while the offended holds on to the offense. I know it is hard to let it go, I know you were hurt by it, but it is essential you do this for your emotional and mental health. The offense becomes a burden as time goes by, one that holds you down. You must drop every burden of offense and hurt to become free again. You can only receive the healing from God after forgiving the person wholeheartedly.

Letting Go of the Hurt

After forgiveness, it is time to let go of the hurt. Forgiveness makes it easier to do that. You let go of hurt by releasing the one who hurt you from the 'prison of offense'; you put them in your heart. When you let go of hurt you feel free.

Submitting to God

By submitting to God, you put your absolute trust in Him, you allow Him to work on you. You give Him the reins; you allow Him to take over. Just as the doctor's patients trust Him and allow Him to work on them, you should also trust God and allow Him to work on you. Submitting to Him also means you trust His judgement, so you do whatever he asks you to do. This is because you know he has your best interest at heart, he cares for you, and is more than willing to give you peace.

"When fear knocks on the door of your mind, let the light of God's word attend to it at the door. Get God's word on every situation in your life."

CONFRONTING THE BEAST

DEALING WITH FEAR AND ANXIETY

Fear and anxiety are an evil duo; while one ties you to the past, the other ensures you are hindered from making any reasonable advancement. You are constantly afraid that things will go badly for you, so you would rather not make any moves.

The harassment that comes from fear is a huge one. Fear causes "mind paralysis", a situation where someone literally stops making any conscious advancement or even think about it. Someone that suffered betrayal from a person they really loved and trusted, shut their heart against anything that has to do with love again; not necessarily because they're being mean, but because of the fear of having to face betrayal again.

Over time, if this fear is not properly dealt with, it becomes a stronghold that places certain restrictions on the person's life.

The Bible calls fear a spirit, a spirit that sponsors bondage.

"For ye have not received the spirit of bondage again to fear." **Romans 8 :15 KJV**

"For God hath not given us the spirit of fear." **2Timothy 1:7 KJV.**

Fear is demonic, it restrains and constrains its victims from going beyond a certain point. No matter how hard they try, they just can't move beyond the mental restriction.

Fear in its subtility creeps in as something casual, then mutates into a strong controlling force that will later be dictating how far a person can go and what the person can do with their own life. Fear is a terrible tyrant. There are over 100 places the phrase "fear not" is mentioned in the Bible.

A lady was betrayed by her lover. It's a genuine case of hurt. She's has been seriously wronged. But, if this hurt and the accompanying pain is not properly dealt with and resolved, it can later result in something more dangerous than the initial pain.

If not handled well, fear will creep in and you will find the same person that used to be cheerful and loving, suddenly become mean, cynical, and suspicious. A person such as this will suspect anyone, even those with very good intentions. Underneath these strange manifestations lies the real issue- fear of being betrayed again.

There are things that reinforce the hold of fear, chief among them is the habit of constantly thinking about the events that caused hurt. Constantly refreshing your memory with images, people, and things that caused you pain will only consolidate the fear of such pain. Deliverance starts with doing away with the memory of such negative events. Prominent among the several reasons fear is dangerous is because fear is anti-faith. Fear works contrary to faith. Meanwhile, without faith it is impossible to please God nor receive anything from Him.

"But without faith it is impossible to please Him: for he that cometh to God must believe…" **Hebrews 11:6 KJV**

"If any of you lack wisdom, let Him ask of God, that giveth to all men liberally, and upbraideth not; and it shall be given Him.

But let him ask in faith, nothing wavering. For he that wavereth is like a wave of the sea driven with the wind and tossed. For let not that man think that he shall receive any thing of the Lord". -**James.1:5 -7** KJV

The Stronghold of Fear

A stronghold is a mental conditioning whereby people think in a particular negative direction and their lives automatically go in that direction.

One of the prominent ways the enemy operates is to create a stronghold in a person's mind by establishing a certain mindset. The person starts living and operating by such a mindset and that gives direction to their lives.

A young lady watched her mom lose two husbands, including her own dad. Then, she entertained the thought process of what if such should happen to her. She constantly thought about this until fear crept into her mind. It got to a point when she became convinced that there was no way she would escape the misfortune that her mom endured. She lived constantly with this fear so much so, that when she met good prospects, she suspected they were going to die soon. Can you imagine that! What man is going to marry a woman that's constantly thinking he is going to die?

She was hindered from advancing towards marriage until the fear was dealt with.

How to Break the Bond of Fear

The tactic of fear is to fix your mind on the things that consolidate its existence. That is, it preoccupies your mind with the things that will further strengthen its existence.

A boy attempted a high jump at the tender age of 13, he fell while trying to lift himself and cross to the other side. The other kids laughed at him, and he was seriously embarrassed. He never made any attempt around high jumping again.

When he got to college, he was encouraged to engage in high jumping again. He finally decided to try, but every time he came close to jumping, he remembered the sad event that happened some years ago and gave in to fear. He was never able to jump until he opened up to someone that told him what his challenge was and showed him how to overcome it.

To break the bond of fear, you must take your mind away from things that constantly remind you of the fear. Thoughts and images are going to spring up in your mind, you have to persistently dodge them no matter how many times they show up in your mind. Giving attention to them will only create a problem.

Fill up your mind with God's word for your life. God's word will act as antivirus against the virus called fear. When fear raises its ugly head, you counter it with what the word of God says. Don't give room to fear in your life.

Demystify Fear

You must demystify fear in your thinking. You must look beyond the lies it keeps telling you.

One of the ways to demystify fear and do away with its grip

is to identify events as totally separate circumstances. That something happened in the past doesn't mean it has to happen again; then and now are not the same.

Fear will attempt to bait you by saying the event will go the same way as the last time. It's a lie. The enemy is a master liar, that's why we counter Him and His lies with God's truth.

A woman who lost her pregnancy doesn't mean she has to believe the lie that she will lose the next one. These are separate events. Totally distinct events: and the outcome is not automatically the same. You can influence the outcome through prayer and faith in God.

"For verily I say unto you, that whosoever shall say unto this mountain, Be thou removed, and be thou cast into the sea; and shall not doubt in His heart, but shall believe that those things which he saith shall come to pass; he shall have whatsoever he saith". - **Mark 11: 23** KJV

To break the bond of fear, you must take charge of your life. Fear and anxiety will suggest to you that things will go wrong no matter what you do. That's a lie! Never believe such, not even for a second. When you take charge of your life, you can dictate how you want every event in your life to go. You have that much power by the authority that's in Christ Jesus. You can influence the outcome of things in your life.

A previously negative case can be altered and straightened. You can influence how they will go. Stand up and rise above the present limitation that fear has placed you in.

Switch on the Light

Have you ever walked in the dark in an area you are not familiar with before? How easy was it for you to navigate around? It couldn't have been smooth. Darkness impairs sight. You stumble and fall into diverse things along the way when there is no light. Fear is the work of the enemy, and it thrives in darkness.

Everyone knows the solution to darkness; introduce light, and there will be an abundance of illumination. This is what you do to fear and the things sponsoring it in your life, they are works of darkness, it is your responsibility to introduce light there and watch them vanish.

God's word is light to your path.

"Thy word is a lamp unto my feet, and a light unto my path". -**Psalms 119:105** KJV

Get God's word in those areas where fear seems to be tormenting you. Fear likes ignorance, ignorance causes it to thrive. The bringing in of knowledge will undo the effect of fear.

Alot of people are afraid of what God has dealt with on their behalf already. Imagine being afraid of what doesn't exist? I have found out that something doesn't need to exist or be real for it to scare you or to cause fear. Many things that do not exist cause all manners of fear for different people. It is incredible.

Many things people are afraid of will not come to pass because they do not exist.

Get your life saturated with God's word.

A lady had an abortion at a point in her life, and since then she has been tormented by the fear of not being able to have a child again. She used to see her fear everywhere, whether she was sleeping or awake. Now, this is not to support abortion but to show you how fear of what is not true can still be a very potent form of bondage. This lady went about with that fear for a long time, sad and depressed because of the fear that she would not give birth again.

Notice that I didn't say the doctor told her so. No, no one said that to her, she just conceived the thought and before she knew what was happening it had become a stronghold of fear.

About a year and half after that, she gave birth. She just wasted her time indulging in worry over what was not there.

When fear knocks on the door of your mind, let the light of God's word attend to it at the door. Get God's word on every situation in your life.

For instance, there are young women already afraid that no man will find them good enough to consider marriage with them. Can you imagine that! This is a common fear. For some of them, it makes them lower their standards, and they begin to do things that are really demeaning just to get validation. It's really sad.

Instead of worrying about your health, why don't you see what God's word says about it?

God's word says you are already healed because Jesus took on your sickness. You do not need to believe the lies of fear that all hope is lost on your matter. That is not true.

"But he was wounded for our transgressions, he was bruised for our iniquities: the chastisement of our peace was upon Him; and with His stripes we are healed". -**Isaiah 53:5 KJV**

"When the even was come, they brought unto Him many that were possessed with devils: and he cast out the spirits with His word, and healed all that were sick: That it might be fulfilled which was spoken by Esaias the prophet, saying, Himself took our infirmities, and bare our sicknesses". -**Matthew 8.16 -17 KJV**

Fear will mess you up big if you accommodate it. It will cause a really big mess around your life if you allow it.

Resist fear by introducing the knowledge of God's word concerning your situation and your fear will disappear.

"Walking in victory over your struggles requires making tough choices. One of those choices is the willingness to choose to focus on the good things God is doing in your life."

BAGGAGE

DEALING WITH THE MEMORIES OF THE PAST

Hurt usually promotes stagnation. They are closely associated.

On your journey to newness there will be many times that the memory of sad events of the past, mistakes, and hurts will haunt you. The winning strategy is not to pay attention to them. Minding them will only cause you more pain and distract you from the things you are trying to achieve.

God knows how important our thought-life is, so he gave us a guideline.

"Finally, brethren, whatsoever things are true, whatsoever things are honest, whatsoever things are just, whatsoever things are pure, whatsoever things are lovely, whatsoever things are of good report; if there be any virtue, and if there be any praise, think on these things". - **Philippians 4:8 KJV**

The strength of hurt is in the memory. When you decide to totally ignore them when they come to your mind, you are liberating yourself from the stronghold of hurt.

There are people that summoned the courage to let go of the whole matter, they put their confidence in God, but were later ambushed with the memory of the past. They didn't resist it; and, by its naturally persistent nature, they fell for the bait and got distracted from their incredible journey.

The memory of hurt has nothing positive to offer anyone. Instead, it destabilizes your balance and focus. Stories abound of people that became hypertensive because they kept overthinking the memory of the past and allowed it to cause damage to their health. Thinking about the hurt of the past will only fix your mind on the past.

Concentrate on the Bright Side

Walking in victory over your struggles requires making tough choices. One of those choices is the willingness to choose to focus on the good things God is doing in your life. In all fairness, this can be tough, but it guarantees the safety of your mental health and helps you to focus on seeing God's works in your life.

When people are going through a season of hurt, they tend to only think about the negative events around their lives, totally ignoring the beautiful things God is still doing in their lives. Your husband left you and the kids, that's a bad experience. But you and the kids have never been stranded since then, somehow God keeps blessing you to meet all your needs. You can't explain the provisions, but you definitely know that you are being sustained somehow. This is the Lord showing you, His goodness. Don't feel depressed and say nothing is good in your life, there are quite a number of good things going on for you. Don't allow depression and bitterness get you to the point that you feel God doesn't care about you nor is he doing enough for you. None of us can say God is not good to us.

"The LORD is good to all: and His tender mercies are over all His works". -**Psalms 145:9 KJV**

"Bless the LORD, O my soul, and forget not all His benefits". -**Psalms 103: 2 KJV**

When people allow the hurt, they are going through to sway their emotions, they start becoming ungrateful, taking the blessings of God for granted. They become "blind" to all he is doing for them.

If you look away from the pain of your hurt, you will realize how much God has been good to you. That you are even alive is evidence of His goodness towards us.

There will be a persistent pull by the memory of events from your past with the aim to hinder you from moving past your past. Mistakes and the wrong choices you made in the past will sometimes haunt you. Dwelling on them will make you indirectly import the negativity of the past into your present. So, instead of you looking forward, you will find yourself living out the realities of the past.

When the thoughts come, you remind yourself that God cares for you, and he has a beautiful plan in place to take care of you. You must convince yourself that all things will work together for your good because God is working things out in your favor.

4 WAYS TO OVERCOME PRESSURES FROM YOUR PAST

1. Mental Disconnection

To effectively handle the pulling from your past you need to create a mental disconnection. That means, undergoing a mental transformation where you affirm to yourself that you have evolved from your past self. This is intentional work that has to be done thoroughly. You know it sounds funny when you can vividly remember your involvement with certain things and certain people in the past and yet, here you are claiming it is not the same person. It may even appear like you are living in denial.

However, it is not denial nor falsehood, it is mind renewal. For this to be effective, there must be an overhauling and an upgrade of your thought pattern. You need to assure yourself that God loves you so much and he is working things out for your favor. He is fighting for you and pleading your cause. It's crucial for you to have the right thinking at this moment because you will see the manifestation of your thought pattern. The Bible says as a man thinks in His heart, that's how he is.

"For as he thinketh in His heart, so is he.."**Proverbs 23:7 KJV**

2. Forgiveness

Nothing brings back the memory of the past like "unforgiveness". A person that hasn't let go of the past by forgiving those that caused hurt to them in the past will constantly struggle with the thoughts and memories of these people. Forgiveness brings about liberty. You become free of the "unforgiveness" that was tying you to the past. You now live as though you were never hurt or offended. Your heart will be so peaceful. This is because you are letting God take charge of your life. You have stopped fighting for yourself. Forgiveness indicates that you trust God enough and you are letting Him deal with the matter however he sees fit.

3. Lifestyle Upgrade

Constantly upgrading ourselves helps to bring out the best in us. Aside from that, one major way to respond to hurt from the past is to strive to be a better edition of yourself. One way to improve yourself is to get closer to God, get to know more about God. When you cultivate intimacy with God, you start finding peace all around. Challenges and problems start giving way because the Lord will go ahead of you to make crooked place straight.

"Acquaint now thyself with Him and be at peace: thereby good shall come unto thee. Receive, I pray thee, the law from His mouth, and lay up His words in thine heart. If thou return to the Almighty, thou shalt be built up...". -**Job 22:21-23 KJV**

There is a tremendous advantage that comes with knowing God, you develop spiritual capacity to weather any storm of life. As God starts rubbing off on you, you start learning His principles and applying them to your life, this is a sure way to a life of perpetual victory and progress.

Take advantage of this season, instead of allowing depression to gain entrance into your life, resolve to grow spiritually. You may decide to cultivate a stronger prayer life. You can read more. You may join a support group of people that will reinforce you and make you stronger.

4. Physical Disconnection from People and Things that Hurt You

It is not a wise posture to seek a new life and still maintain affinity with people responsible for your hurt. This doesn't in any way mean you haven't forgiven them; it means you have moved on with your life.

Depending on what the matter is, even if there will later be a reconnection, you first need that space to work on yourself and your mental health.

In the case of separation in marriage (without outright divorce), there is still a need for that space to reflect on things, work on yourself and pray more.

It's essential for any possibility of a healthy "reunion".

Emphasis on Self-improvement

As I mentioned earlier, general life upgrade is an effective response to hurt and pain from the past.

I'm reiterating this to lay emphasis on its importance.

When a person develops themselves after a season of hurt, their personal growth brings about an amplified capability as a result of the transformation. They have an inner energy to handle what seemed bigger than them before. Their spiritual wiring is now stronger than what the problem is, making it easy for them to handle it effectively. Spiritual transformation brings an all-round improvement to every area of one's life.

"...but the people that do know their God shall be strong and do exploits". **Daniel 11:32**

When you experience a personal upgrade as a result of the illumination from God's word, you will begin to have a better perspective about things. This better perspective produces a better response overall.

Understanding God's Template for Forgiveness and Offense

A man named Peter asked Jesus about how many times he could accommodate being wronged before taking offense. Jesus told Him 70 in 7 places, that's 490 times. Peter was probably taken aback. I would have been too. I guess Peter had someone seriously getting on His nerves and he was planning to give Him a piece of His mind or something more than that before Jesus burst His bubble.

Here is the thing, the idea of the 490 times actually means to forgive ahead before you are wronged. It means not to accommodate offense at all in any case. You can't possibly note down the 200th time a person wronged you!

Naturally, we generally have issues with this approach, but when we understand that God didn't make this recommendation for His sake but for ours, it will help our understanding of it.

Offense does something terrible to the heart, this is what God is trying to shield us from. The danger of offense is largely tilted to the person holding on to it.

The reason people struggle with the idea of not keeping offense is because they somehow feel those that offend them do not deserve their forgiveness. They may not, but God does. God is not asking you to forgive them because they deserve it, we forgive those that wronged us because God says so. If God is to keep track of our own personal wrongdoings towards Him it will greatly outweigh the list of all our offenders combined.

"You must deliberately release the sources of hurt from your mind. By doing this you would have closed a major door that can lead you back into what you are striving to fight off."

LOOKING INTO GOD'S MIRROR II
MIND RECONFIGURATION

The most suitable response to the spillover effect created by negative circumstances is a reconfiguration of your thoughts and mindset to align with what God says about you in His word.

As I mentioned earlier, the usual aftermath of a negative situation is to create a distorted image of who you really are. It's a distorted perception that makes you see yourself lower than God intends you to be.

The most potent measure to eradicate this distorted view is to install a new thought process. We are all products of our thoughts. The Bible says as a man thinks in his heart, so he is. That's true. You are not going to go beyond the limitation of your thoughts. You won't excel beyond the ceiling you have placed upon your life through your thinking. This is how essential your thought is to your well-being.

Your thoughts have a way of attracting the things that are consistent with it to your life. You just find your life going in the direction of your most consistent thought. If you think you are not worth much, you start having experiences that will show that to you.

The idea of reconfiguration is for you to make a 180-degree turn away from your current negative thought. You must change your mind set about yourself.

This is the beginning of a new life for you.

Making a U-turn: Renewing Your Mind

For as he thinketh in His heart, so is he... -**Proverb 23: 7** KJV

Changing your mindset is deliberate work. It requires intentional effort for it to be effective.

You change your mindset and thinking by substituting what the negative things that people and circumstances have made you believe about yourself for the actual things God says about you in His word.

You will have to choose between the words you want to believe about yourself; the lies from people and circumstances, or the truth about you from your maker. When you choose to believe what God says about you, you need to start deliberately substituting your current negative vocabularies for God's word about you.

Instead of thinking and saying you are worthless, you say you are a treasure. Instead of thinking you do not deserve anyone's attention, you constantly remind yourself of the absolute love of God for you. He says he has engrafted you in His palm. He says he has numbered the hairs on your head.

"Behold, I have graven thee upon the palms of my hands
Isaiah 49.16 KJV

Can you imagine how much love and attention he gives to you? It's a whole lot. When you consider God's word for your life, you suddenly realize that you have been feeding your mind with the wrong information. You need to change that.

As you continue to think and say the right things from God's word about yourself, you need to deliberately shut out negative words.

People may say things that will bring back the memory of your past. Their intention may be to lure you back into the thinking of the past. You must avoid such bait.

Whenever something comes up that makes you want to think something negative about yourself, realize that it's time to increase or double the positive things you have been thinking and saying about yourself.

Dealing with Self-doubt

Self-doubt refers to a situation where a person has absolutely no confidence in themselves or in their potential. This negative feeling is an aftermath of one or more negative experiences. It is so strong that a person starts doubting things they used to be sure about. If a beautiful woman got dumped several times by men that used to cherish her, after a while she may start doubting whether she's truly beautiful. An intelligent person may start questioning her intelligence after making choices that resulted in bad experiences.

If this is not addressed, it will deteriorate to a point where the person expresses self-doubt about everything they want to do. The danger of this is that nothing significant can be achieved with this kind of posture. The person with this mindset will self-sabotage herself and her plans because of that mindset of doubt.

A person struggling with self-doubt will be and feel undervalued and underappreciated. People usually rate us based on how we carry ourselves. If you go about with self-doubt, no one will value you nor consider you for anything significant, whether marriage, business deal, promotion, jobs, etc.

The solution here will be to take an inventory of the general activities in your life. Your single objective here is to look for the times God has enabled you to achieve something. You have to carefully recall your past victories. If you set out to look for negativity you will see plenty of it. That's looking in the wrong direction.

There's a story in the Bible of a guy named David facing the biggest challenge he had ever faced in His entire little life. He offered to fight the famous Goliath of Gath, one that had been a champion of many battles long before David was born. Of course, David's volunteering to fight Him came with confidence or some uneducated courage. The king couldn't hide His doubt in David and told Him he was no match for the fiery giant. It was at this point that David courteously called to remembrance the victories God gave Him in the past; how he killed wild beasts in the wilderness. He ended up winning the battle against Goliath.

When faced with a challenge or a situation that is stirring up doubt in you so much that you are beginning to accept it as reality, it's time to call to remembrance all the battles the Lord has helped you to win and the things he has enabled you to accomplish in the past no matter how insignificant they seem.

Your past achievements will stir up confidence and courage in you. They are testimonies of your survival. You might have even survived something bigger than this in the past, yet you are full of self-doubt. You might have achieved something significant before but now because of the circumstances and your recent experience you are doubting yourself to the point of settling for mediocrity. You need to roll out your past exploits. That is the badge of the inherent greatness God has placed in you. It is an assurance that you will overcome your current situation.

Hope Therapy

There is some sort of positive connection between hope and endurance. When hope is high, your endurance level goes up, and when hope is low, your ability and willingness to endure comes down. Hence, when trying to get people to endure a particular thing, they are usually offered some kind of hope as motivation because there is a link between hope and endurance.

Based on the faithfulness of God, having hope leads to success. Those that threw in the towel without accomplishing what they desired were short on hope. People quit on hope before they physically quit. When someone stops hoping it is only a matter of time before they give up on whatever they are holding on to.

You've got to stir up your hope in God; look into His word and see that there is more to your life and your journey than some negative episode. The Bible says those that call upon God shall not be put to shame. You won't be able to weather the storm of the period of pain and gruesome betrayal if you don't have enough hope that God is working things out for you. Your hope in God for a better day is what will keep you going when all you see is gloom.

"Be of good courage, and he shall strengthen your heart, all ye that hope in the LORD". -**Psalms 31:24 KJV**

Hope is similar to faith; it is an assurance that something will turn out in a positive way when there is absolutely no sign of such a view.

The person that will rise past a period of gloom must arm themself with tHis tool.

Closing the Backdoor

There is a backdoor principle in military warfare. It is a battle strategy in which an army attempts to strike its enemy using the weakest link when the link is unguarded.

This strategy is instructive, you must ensure the backdoor of your life is closed with respect to what you are dealing with. If you are not careful, what you have dealt with will attempt to sneak back into your life and you will be back to the low point.

When reconfiguring your mind, watch out for the backdoor. This is one way that may be used to undo all your efforts to move past your current situation.

Close the door on offense, bitterness, and anger.

If after you have started working on yourself you begin to entertain these toxic feelings, you are setting yourself up. You may not see the results of all your efforts.

How do you recognize bitterness?

It is that state of mind that willfully holds on to angry feelings, ready to take offense, able to break out in anger at any moment.

If you still have any feeling of resentment toward those that hurt you or things that caused you to hurt, you are leaving a dangerous door open. It's not safe. While I concede that it could be tough to let go, when you realize that you are the one on the receiving end if you hold on to offense, it will be much easier to let go.

You must deliberately release the sources of hurt from your mind. By doing this you would have closed a major door that can lead you back into what you are striving to fight off.

"Finding newness is about discovering the essence of your life; something worth living for. When you realize that you are not just a random person on earth, that you are someone with enough goodness that will be a blessing to the world and that God has a specific plan for your life, your outlook to things changes."

8

NEWNESS
DECIDING TO LIVE AGAIN

For I know the thoughts that I think toward you, saith the LORD, thoughts of peace, and not of evil, to give you an expected end -**Jeremiah 29.11** KJV

The Bible instructs us to walk by faith not by sight. To walk by sight is to make conclusions based on present situations or what you are currently going through. Walking by faith means seeing things from God's perspective even when they don't appear like that.

To walk with the eyes of faith is to take God for His word.

The truth is we all have experienced some pain at some time or been in some not so good situations. Our postures and responses at those times indicate what we fix our gaze on; it shows whether we are walking by faith (standing on God's word regardless of the situation) or we are walking by sight (letting the circumstances dictate our attitude).

God's word is sure. His character is consistent with His word. He has never gone back on His word nor broken His promises to anyone in the History of mankind. His promise to you regardless of what you're currently facing is that He will give you a beautiful end. We must choose to believe God's word.

You should be familiar with the story of Ruth, the lady from Moab. She married one of the sons of Naomi. When the two sons died, it was it was a difficult time for them. The wife of the other son returned back to her people. Ruth on the other hand, decided to take the adventurous journey of faith; she returned with Naomi to Bethlehem. She later married Boaz, a wealthy man who cared deeply for her. Jesus came to the world as a descendant of that union. Ruth that was once sad, hurt, and lonely became an ancestor to the Lord Jesus because God wasn't through with her despite the circumstances.

God is not through with you either. It is true that your pain runs deep. You may be at a point where all you see is hurt, pain, betrayal, and hopelessness. Yet, you don't have to let them decide the final outcome of your life. Your life is in God's hand, and you need to put your confidence in His ability to turn things around for you.

Having felt the intense pain of hurt, I know exactly how painful it can be. I'm in no way downplaying or underestimating the brutal sting of hurt especially from those close to us. Nonetheless, despite the pain, the confusion and sorrow of your heart, you can't afford to end your journey in that fashion. There is more to your life than the chapters of hurt. You can, if you so decide, to rise from the mud of pain and regret, make a U-turn, and begin to walk the path of newness by allowing God to fix you and fix the situation. God specializes in fixing things and people considered hopeless.

When you refuse to move on from hurt, you are giving other

people more power over your life than they deserve. When you insist on holding on to offense and hurt, you are passively relinquishing to others the authority that should be exclusively yours. Nothing should be given such dominion over you.

When you decide to embrace newness by allowing God to fix things in His own way instead of holding onto offense and pain, you will realize how much you can still get from life.

Even in the midst of a dark moment, you must embrace hope. Don't allow the enemy to deceive you into hopelessness. With God all things are possible.

There are no hopeless situations with God, people just grow hopeless about certain matters.

Here is what the Bible says;

For there is hope of a tree, if it be cut down, that it will sprout again, and that the tender branch thereof will not cease. Though the root thereof wax old in the earth, and the stock thereof die in the ground; Yet through the scent of water, it will bud and bring forth boughs like a plant -**Job14:7-9 KJV**. Your situation is not hopeless, you just need to reach out for the brook of water, and you will rise again.

Don't allow painful situations to deceive you into thinking that is all there is to life. You can still go on from here to a beautiful life the way God planned for you. When you choose to believe God instead of quitting, when you allow Him to steer the wheel instead of struggling with Him, you will see that God in His mercy will lead you to your desires.

You could have made serious mistakes in the past. You might have laid down your life for people who later paid you back with wickedness. It's possible you have experienced betrayal from someone you gave your all to. You might even have lost loved ones to the cold hand of death. Regardless of the nature of the hurt, you still don't have to allow it to control your life and bring it to a complete halt, instead you let God in and allow Him to give you fresh start.

Stagnancy is often associated with hurt because hurt keeps you holding on to what happened in the past. The loss of a loved one may have you not wanting to live again. You may not want to trust any human being again because of the betrayal you experienced from those close to you. And, you might have shut your heart to love because of how someone repaid your love with indescribable hurt. Regardless of the nature of the hurt and its intensity, you can rise up from there to a life of total newness in God.

On the path of newness, you will find someone that will treasure your trust. You will meet people that will genuinely care about and provide support for you. Much more is available when you decide to surrender to Jesus to fix the matter.

The Essence of Your Life

Before I formed thee in the belly, I knew thee; and before thou camest forth out of the womb I sanctified thee, and I ordained thee...-**Jeremiah1:5** KJV

It is both delighting and refreshing to realize the love of God and His plans predate your existence. That is, before you came into this world, God had a plan for your life. Before the many setbacks and negative experiences, God already created a perfect plan and purpose for your life. this beautiful plan is what God insists in His word to give you.

The fact that God's plans for us existed before any earthly experience is a truth that is worth emphasizing because, in the face of challenges we tend to forget that God has a glorious plan for us, a plan that is not in any way dependent on your current circumstance.

Have you ever thought of the main reason for your existence on earth? The character of God indicates that He is thorough and intentional about all His endeavors. This means God creating you and bringing you on earth is for an essential purpose. You haven't completed your journey until you achieve that important purpose for which you are on earth and fulfil the plans God has for you.

Finding newness is about discovering the essence of your life; something worth living for. When you realize that you are not just a random person on earth, that you are someone with enough goodness that will be a blessing to the world and that God has a specific plan for your life, your outlook toward things will change. The way you see yourself changes. You receive strength to withstand pain without letting them define you nor your journey because you know God has a specific plan and a genuine intention to bring them to pass. This is the secret of a lasting peace and confidence; knowing that God is deliberate about your life, and that he has a well mapped out plan for you.

Realize that you are not just a random figure that should be lost in the shuffle of humanity. You are created in the image of God for a life of significance. Past mistakes, hurts and series of negative events can't change that.

Reflection, not Regret

Finally, brethren, whatsoever things are true, whatsoever things are honest, whatsoever things are just, whatsoever things are pure, whatsoever things are lovely, whatsoever things are of good report;

if there be any virtue, and if there be any praise, think on these things - **Philippians 4:8 KJV**

God knows how important our thinking is to our entire life. Not just our thinking but the objects of our thoughts, because of that, He gave us certain constraints in an attempt to help us have healthy thoughts which will later have an effect on our lives.

When in a painful position, the natural response is usually a regretful feeling. Such a feeling rarely does anything positive. A regretful feeling, if not contained will create a bigger mess. A better approach is to substitute reflection for regret. As you embark on your journey to newness, you pick vital lessons from the past negative circumstances instead of worrying about them. These lessons will serve as your anchor as you progress, silently informing you on what and whom to engage with and what and whom to avoid.

It is important to note that while we shouldn't deliberately look for negative events, there are invaluable lessons and instructions that we can take from them without accepting the events. **Ecclesiastes 7:14 KJV** -" In the day of prosperity be joyful, but in the day of adversity consider". To consider means to have a deep reflection about a thing with the aim of getting a solid understanding about the matter. This is one of the ways to grow in knowledge. You will realize that you become wiser by pondering on those matters from the past. They open your eyes to see what you weren't seeing clearly at that time. These help to identify pitfalls and know how to avoid them.

Setback or hurt is never the end of a person whose faith is in God. Many times, the difference between those that will end up becoming successful in their pursuit and those that will fall by the wayside is the ability to handle pain and setback without letting it affect their entire life nor bring it to a complete halt. This ability is not just sheer courage but a deep-rooted confidence in the promises of God to make all things work out for your good.

Dust yourself from every disappointment, pain, hurt, or betrayal. Your life is more than some episodes of negative events. You can rise from here to a new beginning. A couple of years from now, you will be very glad you didn't give up. You will be glad that you chose to trust God. Giving up means the end of your journey.

You will be proud of yourself that you didn't throw in the towel even when you were hit the hardest, despite your pain and struggles you still managed to hold on to God and still kept going.

Your story will inspire many, who may later find themselves in your current position. They will draw strength from your faith in God and determination to move on and create a new life for yourself.

This will be the motivation that will encourage them to put their confidence in God.

Resurrection!

It seems betrayal and hurt have been as old as the world itself. There have been abundant stories of betrayals across diverse countries and cultures. A prominent case is that of Jesus and Judas. Judas was a member of the inner circle of Jesus, he betrayed Him by selling Him out to His enemies for some amount of money. He later regretted it and committed suicide.

The surprising thing in this story is that when Jesus resurrected after he was killed and buried, he went to meet His remaining disciples but never mentioned what Judas did or how he was betrayed.

In all the times he spent with the disciples after His resurrection, He never mentioned Judas' betrayal once. He just moved on with the agenda.

This is a major insight. When you "resurrect" you don't talk about those that "killed" you. The proof that you rose up from what they did to you, and you have moved on is that you don't make reference to them or what they did.

The journey to newness starts with forgiveness and forgetting about the past. Forgiving those that wronged us or caused us pain is a major indicator that we have now surrendered the matter into God's hand. When you struggle with offense and bitterness, it shows you are still trying to resolve the issue by yourself. The Bible says the throne of God is built on justice. God is a just God, he will make sure he makes right every wrong, you don't need to do it yourself.

Most times, our approach of handling hurt, and pain is quite different from God's. You may not like His method at first, it may even appear slow, but once you trust the Lord, you have to do it with all your heart in all situations. That means even when you don't understand how He intends to help you out and get justice for you, you still have to put all your trust in Him.

"You are worth more than you think. You are not just one of the many creations of God, you are You- a special creation of God, created and designed by Him for a special purpose, saved by the precious blood of Jesus. God takes special interest in you and all that concerns you. You are special, that's why I liken you to rubies."

RUBIES

YOU ARE MORE THAN WHAT YOU THINK

Since you are precious and honored in my sight, and because I love you, I will give people in exchange for you, nations in exchange for your life. - **Isaiah 43:4 NIV**

You are worth more than you think. You are not just one of the many creations of God, you are You- a special creation of God, created and designed by Him for a special purpose, saved by the precious blood of Jesus. God takes special interest in you and all that concerns you. You are special, that's why I liken you to rubies.

Rubies are rare, precious, and highly valuable gems. They are usually found in metamorphic rocks. Since the gem is embedded in rocks, it's going to be hard to know its value from the surface, especially with the rocks looking all rough and unattractive. So, imagine the ruby looking down on itself, thinking it's just a rock like others and not recognizing its value. Meanwhile, it's something people are looking, digging, and searching for. You really are worth more than you think.

There's a need for you to reconfigure your mind. Start believing you are worth more than what you think. The Lord wouldn't pay special attention to you if you weren't worth it. God, in His awesomeness, made you in His own image. That is priceless. You must constantly remember this, put it in your consciousness that you were made in His image. You are His masterpiece. You are a person of value, a person of worth. You must not have low self-worth. Low self-worth keeps you perpetually depressed and constantly feeling sorry for yourself. A person with low self-worth has the fear of failing so they never try new things, they never step out of the box. They also have this inferiority complex and feeling of inadequacy. This hinders them from making any progress. Living like this just ensures depression and hurt remain constant because, when you do not make any progress, the low self-worth runs deeper. That is why you must never have low self-worth. I understand that your past experiences conditioned you into having such feelings. But you must work on it and recognize your worth. That is what God wants for you.

Knowing your worth will also help you to understand that your past or whatever you have gone through does not devalue you. Your past experiences do not reduce your value. Your value is the blood of Jesus. And that's incredibly high.

There is a need for you to discover your true worth, you must begin to embark on a journey to self-discovery, a journey to discover your true worth.

The Journey to Self-Discovery

You must discover your true value. If the value of a thing is not known, it is underpriced. It is when you know your true worth and present yourself as such that people treat you with respect. When you present yourself as the valuable person that you are, people treat you as a person of value. This discovery is also important in determining how you view yourself, that is, your self-image and worth.

You know, feeling sorry for yourself is a recipe for stagnancy, you just remain at the same spot while the world keeps moving. The sorry feeling makes you unable to see your true worth. When you continue feeling sorry for yourself, your assessment of your true value becomes hazy. It also makes you feel like you can't achieve anything. You know, there is this confidence you exude when you know how valuable you are. When you feel sorry for yourself, you can't do things confidently. Do not allow the hurt you experienced in the past reduce your self-esteem or make you timid, you must boost your self-confidence and stop feeling sorry for yourself. Get rid of that feeling and recognize your worth.

Discover Your Gifts and Talents

What are gifts and talents? You need to look within yourself to discover them. You must know that these gifts and your talents were deposited by God. He would not give them to you if he didn't think you were worth it. He gave them to you for a purpose. This goes further to explain that you were created specifically for that purpose, God doesn't deal with frivolities. He invested a lot in you. Discovering your gifts and talents helps you to increase your self-image-the way you see and value yourself. So, look within yourself. Are there things you enjoy or love doing? Knowing your hobbies or the things you love doing makes it easier for you to find your talents, they usually align. When you check critically, you are going to discover them.

Put the Gift to Good Use

When you get busy using your gifts and talents, you will hardly have time to feel sorry for yourself. Living a purposeful life makes you feel fulfilled. In turn, you become more confident in your abilities and worth. You gradually let go of the hurt and focus on using your abilities. Before you know it, the pain and hurt start receding. You eventually get to a point where you can hold your head up high.

You must ensure that what happened in your past does not affect your present life. It should not affect how you see yourself. It's all in the past. You are special, you are God's masterpiece, loved and specially made by Him. You are a person of worth. There's more to you. Do not feel inferior at any time. Conquer any inferiority complex and disregard what others might say or think, because you, like rubies, are a rare gem.

"There is an immense strength and energy that comes from receiving encouragement from someone that deeply understands your pain and your journey. You understand their pain and you strategically help them to move past it."

BECOMING A BURDEN BEARER

"Blessed be God, even the Father of our Lord Jesus Christ, the Father of mercies, and the God of all comfort, Who comforteth us in all our tribulation, that we may be able to comfort them which are in any trouble, by the comfort wherewith we ourselves are comforted of God." – **2 Corinthians 1: 3 -4 KJV**

One day you will overcome your struggles. Your current hurt and pain will be so distant from your memory that you will have to struggle to recollect them. When you get to tHis point, your new responsibility is to help those that are where you used to be.

There is an immense strength and energy that comes from receiving encouragement from someone that deeply understands your pain and your journey. You understand their pain and you strategically help them to move past it.

This is my own contribution to you. I'm doing this because I've been where you are currently. I'm persuaded that you've got what it takes to move past this present negative experience to a new world of excitement and fulfilment.

Victory First

The strength of your testimony and the ability to help others is dependent on your victory over your struggles. Overcoming your struggles and moving on from your pain earns you the authority to help others in their own struggles.

When you are able to move on from your hurt and still attain your desired point, you will be able to show others with similar issues the required steps to navigate their paths.

Your survival is not just for you. Your survival has connections with other things and many other people. There are people that will draw the strength to live on instead of quitting because of your story of survival.

What Does it Mean to be Victorious?

You know the word victorious indicates an underlying battle is being engaged. The good news is that you aren't the one fighting. How do you win if you are not fighting? You can if someone is fighting for you. Your fight is a fight of faith, your weapon of war is your total submission to God and full confidence in His ability to right every wrong for you. You have stopped fighting yet, you are winning.

To be victorious in this case means to overcome the issues that have been the source of pain and hurt for you. It means to come to a point whereby you do not look like what happened to you in the past or what you are currently going through. It means to heal completely, unless you show your wound to people, they may not know that you were once hurt, betrayed, or deserted. You do all this by submitting your life to Jesus and allowing Him to take care of every matter. The Bible says Jesus is your advocate, the one that pleads your cause. A person that fights for your rights. Let Him handle the matter. When you try to heal by your strength, you deepen the wound. When you try to fight by yourself you expose yourself to injury. Your victory is in allowing your advocate to plead your cause.

"My little children, these things write I unto you, that ye sin not. And if any man sin, we have an advocate with the Father, Jesus Christ the righteous". – **1 John 2:1 NIV**

When you allow God to help you out, you will find ultimate healing, what seemed lost will be restored. Your scar by then won't be a sign of pain anymore but a symbol of an incredible trust in God.

Your first step to total victory is to stop fighting by yourself and let God in on the matter. You then cease from your struggles, and you enter into rest.

Your vocabulary and general speaking have a way of reflecting whether you have crossed over from hurt and pain to healing and peace through Christ. If you still complain and grumble about your issues, it means you still have not totally submitted the case to God. There is a peace and assurance of comfort that comes when a person genuinely surrenders a matter to God.

Someone that went through a phase of hurt and pain and has now moved on from it is totally different from someone still struggling with the phase. Their language shows positivity. They are thankful and joyful and doesn't speak negativity because they know God is working things out in their favor.

The Turning Point

The turning point is that defining moment when you do all you can to move past the trauma of hurt and the accompanying pains. It is a crucial phase. That's the time some people give up because of the magnitude of the hurt. Some even engage in some extreme things because they weren't able to bear the pain.

At this very important period of your life, when things are not looking very bright nor going the way you had envisioned it, you need to have faith in God. You have to convince yourself that the pain will pass, and you will still be standing strong according to what God's word says concerning you. Pour your heart out to God, don't give up on Him, he will surely come through for you. He will never let your feet be moved.

"I will lift up mine eyes unto the hills, from whence cometh my help. My help cometh from the LORD, which made heaven and earth. He will not suffer thy foot to be moved..." **Psalms 121:1-3 KJV**

Gold in Distress

Have you heard the story of an old poor farmer that was forced to leave His house by the king to go to an extremely rural place? His only neighbors in this new residence were animals. After feeling so bad for a number of days he decided to make the best he could of the situation. So, he started farming, and one day while digging, His hoe touched something strange. The man stumbled on gold! This became His ticket out of poverty. He became the envy of those that once hurt and oppressed Him.

Can you imagine what would have been going on in the

mind of the old farmer when he was forcefully chased out of His own house? He would have felt powerless, the pain would have been very deep. Can you also imagine Him getting to the new residence, realizing how bad things are for Him and finally killed Himself. Had he done that, we wouldn't be drawing insight from His story. No one will ever talk about it, no one will be interested in hearing it. The reason is because people are looking for motivation, some kind of encouragement to help them face their struggle. They are hoping they could learn a thing or two from someone that will assure them that things can still be better. This is why people only choose to listen to stories of people that refused to give up.

There is gold in your distress as well. Maybe not a physical bag of gold but some precious insight, some invaluable understanding. Some opportunities in disguise will give room for self-development. It could be anything.

I have learned that no matter how messy the situation is, if one can look deeper with a positive lens, you will soon find that something good will come out of the situation.

Stories abound of folks that discovered their greatness when hit the hardest. Many became stronger, some got closer to God and found His love for them, some got a business idea in the midst of the pain. Someone published their story as a book and made millions while impacting lives alongside.

I heard of a man that went to jail; during His jail time he started telling other inmates funny stories and jokes just to lift their spirits. They all told Him he was very funny; funnier than many comedians they had seen on television. The guy noted their compliment. When His jail term was over, he decided to give His life meaning, he decided to get close to God, and talked to a few people that could help Him become a better person. After that, he started out as a standup comedian.

There are precious things even in unpleasant places.

While no one should deliberately wish to experience hurt and pain, there is invaluable treasure that can be obtained from it if we approach the situation with the right posture.

Burden of Intercession

The word burden already gives a hint that it is not something fun. Yes, it is not. Bearing someone's burden means putting yourself in their shoes, feeling their pain and helping them to go through it.

Some matters are more complicated than others.

You need to learn to engage in intercession for those you are sharing their burden. To intercede means to pray deliberately for them concerning specific matters. These people may not even be aware that you are doing such for them but the influence and the effects of it will be so palpable that they note that something is definitely changing for them.

Sometimes you pray for them for the fortitude to bear the hurt or pain they are going through. God has a way of wiring a capacity in us to bear things that are bigger than us. Make no mistake, none of us is superman or superwoman. Superman is a myth created to entertain people. It's at best a fantasy. We are all human, with limited strength and abundant limitations. We all have our thresholds of how much we can bear. When we come against certain things that overwhelm our threshold, unless we get some reinforcement, it's a matter of time before we crumble. I really think it is a foolish thing and a sign of ignorance to conclude that people are weak because of the way they react to their hurt and pain, especially if you have no idea of what they are going through.

Whenever we are at this point, this is when we must, as a matter of urgency, tap into a higher power for reinforcement. This is what prayer does for us. It serves as an invite to God to give us some supernatural aid. It helps us to go through overwhelming situations without losing ourselves in the process.

"I sought the LORD, and he heard me, and delivered me from all my fears.

They looked unto Him and were lightened: and their faces were not ashamed.

This poor man cried, and the LORD heard Him, and saved Him out of all His troubles". **Psalms 34: 4-6 KJV**

When you intercede for someone going through hurt and pain, you are holding them up, you are reinforcing them.

And I think our society would be much better if we had more people holding others going through a painful period in their lives up in prayer rather than gossiping about them or judging their choices.

Frequent Communication

Those going through hurt need someone to talk to whether they realize it or not. It's even better if it is a person that knows exactly how they are feeling. That's where you come in. Your words will be so impactful on them because you know exactly what they are going through, having been there yourself. Aside from that, you are an embodiment of what they are hoping to attain.

Communication is powerful, it is essential to our being. We are created in such a way that it will be impossible to survive without communication.

Meanwhile, when people are going through a difficult time, one of the things they do is to cut off communication with others. Some just want to be alone to process things, some are afraid to share the matter with others for fear of how they will handle it. You will be helping a lot by finding a common ground to communicate with a person going through a difficult experience. They sometimes may act like they don't want you around, but they will later appreciate your concern once they see that it is genuine.

Restoring their Enthusiasm

The first thing that a person going through hurt, and pain will lose is enthusiasm toward everything. They no longer find things interesting. They are not excited about anything; they feel their worlds have crashed down.

When working with them as a burden bearer, you need to be keen and skillful to draw back their enthusiasm in everyday life.

Anyone that committed suicide must have exhausted their bank of enthusiasm. Enthusiasm is a sign of life; lack of it signals an underlying problem that must be resolved urgently.

I met a woman that lost her husband. She told me that after the tragedy, she had no will to continue living. That is a huge one.

Well, the way out for her was to channel all her energy into the company her husband founded before he died. She told herself that her husband must be happy seeing her tireless efforts in the business, that was how she found her enthusiasm again.

Restoring enthusiasm is crucial to restoring the person.

"The scriptures say that if you walk with wise men, you become wise, same way if you walk with strong people, you become strong. Company with the strong so that you too can become strong. After some time, when you look back at your past, you will have a lot to thank God for because in your future, you will have totally recovered from the hurt you experienced in the past."

11

BEING IN THE COMPANY OF THE STRONG

FINDING THE RIGHT ENVIRONMENT

"Two are better than one...If either of them falls down, one can help the other up. But pity anyone who falls and has no one to help them up." **Ecclesiastes 4:9-10 NIV**.

Judy was heartbroken. She didn't know how to move on from her past. She had overcome the fear of trying again but she still didn't know how to go about it until she had the help of her friends. Overcoming her fear was something she never thought she could do but her friend, Lisa, really stood by her. Lisa was there for her, always encouraging her to try again. She always checked on her and prayed with her. There were times Judy was down because the thought of the past was overwhelming, her friend always came through for her. She wouldn't have been able to cope if not for her friend.

Recently, Lisa introduced her to some other friends, people who have their own stories but have been able to move on. They are really nice people; they pray with her and check on her often. Gradually, she got stronger and more positive about the future. On days when she was down and feeling sorry for herself, they were always there for her with their prayers and words of encouragement. She was in the company of the strong, they created the right environment for her to move on from the past.

She has been reflecting a lot these past few days, remembering her past and this has helped her to understand the importance of being with the right people and in the right environment. The friends she used to have contributed a lot to the mess she found herself in. They were so negative, constantly fueling her problem with their words. She could never go to them for help because she was afraid, they would laugh at her. Now, she has wonderful people in her circle who wouldn't judge her for her past but are willing to help her become better.

Like Judy, having the right people in your space can help you to face the future without fear. They encourage and stand by you. They even help to keep you in check, prevent you from feeling sorry for yourself, and pray for you and with you.

To find these kinds of people, you need to be open and admit to yourself that you need people to help you. When you admit that you need help, that's one step closer to finding it. There are some things you need to do in order to get yourself in the company of the strong.

1. Detach from Negative People

It's quite easy to know when we find ourselves in the midst of negative people. Being in the company of negative people hinders progress, in fact, there could even be regression. A person trying to move on from the past doesn't need any bad energy around. So, detach yourself from people who do not know how to ease your burden and make you feel loved while you're working hard to get back on your feet again.

2. Position Yourself for Positive People

Positioning yourself in the right environment will require open-mindedness. You need to understand that everybody is not the same. The fact that you were with some negative people doesn't mean you can't find the right people for you. You need to be open-minded and ready to accept new people in your space. It may be gradual, but it is something you need to do. You must determine in your mind that you're ready to accept new people into your space.

You also need to prayerfully ask God to get you in contact with the people that can help your situation. God answers prayers. There are some people who are committed to helping others heal from hurt as they have also been hurt in the past but were able to heal from it. As a result of their previous experiences and their recovery from it, they know how to help somebody in a similar situation.

Also, when people extend a hand of friendship to you, try to accept it, of course it should be after you're sure of the kind of people they are. The scriptures also advise that we choose our friends carefully. By doing this, you step out of your 'lonely zone". It also helps you to get to know them better, you get to evaluate and see if they are people that fit your purpose of recovery from hurt.

3. Learn to Trust Again

Trust is your belief in the character and ability of an entity/person. You must ensure that you're sure of the person's character before putting your trust in them. This will make it easy for you to trust them.

You must learn to trust people again. It's one thing to find the right people, it's another thing to trust them. The right people can only impact your life if you let them. You must trust them and be willing to accept their help. By trusting them, you heed their counsel and guidelines to an effective recovery. Don't shut yourself off from the world, that will make the healing process slow. Now, I know you may find it hard to do that considering your previous encounter with people but, it is what you need to do to get the right people in your space. Moving with the right people helps you to heal faster. So, you must learn to trust people again.

Being in the right company and environment cannot be overemphasized. It aids progress, and you even get to learn from their experiences and past mistakes. You also get to glean from their strength. The scriptures say that if you walk with wise men, you become wise, same way if you walk with strong people, you become strong. Company with the strong so that you too can become strong. After some time, when you look back at your past, you will have a lot to thank God for because in your future, you will have totally recovered from the hurt you experienced in the past.

"Realize that your future doesn't depend on your past, it depends on God. The fact that you had some negative experiences doesn't mean you can't go from here to a really beautiful life. It all depends on you."

WHERE DO I GO FROM HERE?

YOUR JOURNEY TO A NEW BEGINNING

At every point in our lives as humans we can decide to choose a new beginning no matter what the past looks like.

Having made the decision to look beyond the past and venture into a totally new beginning, there must be a specific destination in view and very clear plans on how to get there.

The challenge sometimes faced by people attempting a new journey in life after a negative episode is that they sometimes don't have a specific destination in mind. They somehow think things will just work out naturally. Meanwhile, life sometimes doesn't share their optimism. So, after encountering one or two hurdles along the way, they give up and never try again.

Where do you want to go from here? You can still be all God made you to be, you just have to know the right things to do and do them with stern determination.

The dreams in your heart can still be lived out.

The first step in determining where to go from here is to identify what brings you fulfilment, what makes you feel alive, and what you can do that will positively impact the world.

When you identify these desires, you then begin to learn proven principles on how to achieve them.

For instance, if you desire a blissful marriage with a loving and godly spouse, it's not beyond your reach, you just need to learn how that can be possible.

Realize that your future doesn't depend on your past, it depends on God. The fact that you had some negative experiences doesn't mean you can't go from here to a really beautiful life. It all depends on you.

On this journey, moving from where you are at the moment to where you desire to be will require absolute teachability; the willingness to be open-minded in order to garner the required knowledge for success in your endeavors. You will need to do some unlearning and relearning.

Leaning on Wise Counsel

On the path to newness, you are going to need a lot of guidance to avoid pitfalls. You need to carefully seek out proven mentors that can help you in this new phase.

"Where no counsel is, the people fall: but in the multitude of counsellors there is safety". -**Proverbs 11:14** KJV

"Without counsel purposes are disappointed: but in the multitude of counsellors, they are established". **Proverbs 15: 22** KJV

The advantage of mentorship is that it guarantees some level of speed. This is because you will be walking with someone that has passed the route you want to venture into. While others are falling into ditches along the way, making series of mistakes beginners make, your own actions are guided, hence you are more balanced.

Things Mentorship will do for You

1. Balance

Once your actions are guided, you are shielded from the common mistakes folks make on that journey. When others are learning through their own mistakes and paying really heavy prices while also wasting their precious time, you are taking proven steps with a minimized error margin.

2. Stability

Though stability is similar to balance, they are not the same.

Stability and balance are two factors that are often equated with one another, but they are quite different. Both concepts take time to fully develop, and the road to achieving them is not always an easy one. It is during this journey that a person may become discouraged and feel like giving up. However, it is important to remember that progress takes time, and it is important to have patience and perseverance. This is where guidance comes into play.

Guidance can provide valuable insight into the process of achieving stability and balance. It can help a person understand the delay between their efforts and the visible outcomes. Without guidance, a person may become frustrated and give up, not realizing that their efforts are actually making a difference. With guidance, a person can stay on track and remain focused on their goals. It can also provide support and encouragement during challenging times.

It is important to stay on track and continue the journey towards stability and balance. Even though it may seem like progress is slow or non-existent, it is important to keep pushing forward. With guidance, a person can gain a better understanding of the process and have a more complete picture of their progress. As they continue to work towards their goals, they will eventually reach a point where stability and balance are achieved. So, remember to stay motivated, have patience, and seek guidance when needed, and you will eventually reap the rewards of your efforts. The mentor, having been in that phase before, can offer invaluable insight to a beginner.

It takes a well-crafted plan to achieve a desired outcome. Like I mentioned earlier, many that seek to create a new life for themselves sometimes do not have a strategic plan on how to go about it. Most times, they just want to move away from the current phase they are in. They soon encounter certain hurdles and since there is no plan on how to circumvent around it, they are hindered from progressing, they soon get frustrated and quit trying again.

Plans are essential if an end result is desired.

Developing Plans and Strategies

"The preparations of the heart in man, and the answer of the tongue, is from the LORD". -**Proverbs 16.1 KJV**

One of the things God does for us after submitting to Him is to give us wisdom on how to move from where we are to our desired destination. This wisdom will be translated into plans. This is very important. Plans that will be devised have to be tailored after a specific result. Some will be long-term while some others will be short-term.

The plans must be interwoven. If someone decides after a period of hurt that they want to have strong financial independence, they may construct a 2 to 5-year plan of becoming debt free or learn how to make investments that would yield a huge dividend. This could be regarded as a long-term goal. If a person decides on this without breaking it down into specific short-term goals, they may never achieve their target. The is because having a decision alone does not birth anything, following up that decision with a suitable action is what produces results.

An appropriate short-term goal could be to get a good financial education; that is, to understand how money works.

This short-term goal will culminate into the desired long-term objective.

A person that went through a divorce may have a long-term goal to remarry. An appropriate short-term goal may be to carefully reevaluate the things that affected the previous marriage. Along with this process of reevaluation will be a deliberate increase of knowledge of how to achieve a blissful marriage. They can start studying books and seeking counsel from people with good results in the area of marriage.

The plans have to be customized; exactly tailored for the specific situation. However, for it to be effective, there must be short-term goals within the overall objective.

Having plans help provide a roadmap toward the desired outcome. It also calls our attention to possible hurdles and difficulties along the way. The idea is not to discourage our venture but to equip us with the appropriate tools to bypass everything standing between us and our goals.

Where there is no plan, people forge ahead with uneducated hope and enthusiasm only to face stiff resistance along the way. Most times, they drop the whole idea of a new life and never make an attempt again.

Attempt to do Something Great

There are two prominent issues commonly associated with folks recovering or going through hurt or a season of pain. As a result of the negative experience, they tend to lower their expectations and settle for something average if not outright mediocrity.

The second thing they struggle with is the fear of failure. This is extremely dangerous as it causes "mind paralysis"; a situation where the person cannot think or carry out any plan to advance for fear she may fail.

Owing to these two closely related problems, often times, people going through this phase don't want to carry out any great tasks. All ambitions and desires would have been relegated to a lower position. They just want to keep existing.

You don't have to follow such a route; you can decide to do things in a totally different manner.

You must attempt to do something huge. That things didn't go the way you planned it in the past doesn't mean it won't work out in the future. We can learn from our mistakes and know that your past doesn't define your future.

If you are going to move from this phase to a better one successfully you will need to separate your past and certain events from who you are now. The fact that you had a failed marriage doesn't mean you are a failure in life. The fact that a person dropped out of school doesn't mean they don't have what it takes to follow things through until a result is achieved. These are very separate matters.

Realizing this will bring a lot of peace of mind and a better perspective.

When you have made a well drafted plan which includes evaluation of past events to extract lessons, you must forge ahead with courage and an unbending determination. Without the duo of courage and determination, not a thing can be achieved.

After much consideration of your plans, you need to go all out. Convince yourself that you have all it takes to accomplish your desire, then go all out to chase them.

Never settle for an average life because of what you are going through.

Regret of Unfulfilled Desires

I have seen a couple of people living with the regret of what they could have done, that they didn't do because they were afraid, they might fail. I really can't say whether you will fail or not in your attempts but what I can say is that not attempting anything at all is failure in itself. Years down the line when you would have overcome this phase, you will look back at many beautiful things you desired that you never reached out for, because of fear. The regret will be enormous.

Despite the hurt and the pain, you are going through, you can still do something great with your life. This negative experience shouldn't put a ceiling on how far you can go. Put your faith in God and watch Him right every wrong done to you.

"You hold the power to redefine your narrative, to shape a future filled with purpose, joy, and resilience. May this journey grant you the wisdom to learn, the strength to endure, and the courage to celebrate the magnificence of your renewed and empowered self. The canvas of your life is yours to paint—a masterpiece in the making, enriched by every color of experience and every stroke of resilience."

CONCLUSION

In the journey from pain to renewal, the lessons learned, and the paths walked are testaments to human resilience. Each step taken, each moment of vulnerability, and each decision made shapes a narrative of growth and transformation.

As we close this chapter, remember that the past does not dictate the future. Your story isn't confined by the trials you've faced; it's enriched by the strength you've gathered. Embrace the courage to dream again, to strive for greatness, and to seek fulfillment. Trust in God's guidance, open your heart to new experiences, and surround yourself with those who uplift and inspire.

The road to a new beginning is not always easy, but it's a journey worth taking. You possess the power to redefine your narrative, to chart a course toward a life of purpose and joy. May this journey bring you the wisdom to learn, the resilience to endure, and the courage to embrace the beauty of a renewed and empowered life.

It's essential to recognize that your journey from pain to newfound strength is a testament to the human spirit's incredible resilience. It's not just about moving on; it's about the transformation that occurs in the process.

Every step you take towards healing, every moment you

embrace vulnerability, and every decision made to rebuild shapes the narrative of your growth. It's not merely about leaving the past behind; it's about learning from it, gathering strength, and embracing the beauty of your evolving story.

Remember, your past doesn't define your future. Your story isn't confined to the struggles you've faced; it's illuminated by the resilience you've shown. Embrace the courage to dream anew, to reach for the extraordinary, and to seek fulfillment in every step you take.

Trust in the guidance of faith, open your heart to new possibilities, and surround yourself with those who support and uplift you. The path to a new beginning may present challenges, but within those challenges lie opportunities for growth and transformation.

You hold the power to redefine your narrative, to shape a future filled with purpose, joy, and resilience. May this journey grant you the wisdom to learn, the strength to endure, and the courage to celebrate the magnificence of your renewed and empowered self. The canvas of your life is yours to paint—a masterpiece in the making, enriched by every color of experience and every stroke of resilience.

AFTERWORD

Thank you for taking the time to read my book, Moving Past the Hurt: Reclaiming Your Identity in Christ. It was a labor of love, and I am grateful for the opportunity to share it with you.

Your support means everything to me, and I hope that the words within these pages have touched your heart and inspired you to reclaim your true identity in Christ.

I would be honored if you could leave a review for my book on Amazon and Goodreads. Your feedback not only helps me as an author, but it also helps other readers discover this book and the message it contains. By sharing your thoughts, you are helping to spread the message of healing and hope to those who may need it.

Don't forget to subscribe to my newsletter to stay updated on new releases, giveaways, and other exciting news.

Together, let's continue to build a community of readers who are passionate about reclaiming their true identity in Christ.

Thank you again for your support.
Cheryl Dyson-Bennett
www.cheryldysonbennett.info

You can also find me on:
Instagram
Facebook
Facebook Group

ABOUT THE AUTHOR

Dr. Cheryl Dyson-Bennett is a highly esteemed life coach, acclaimed author, and sought-after motivational speaker, dedicated to guiding individuals toward realizing their highest potential. As the visionary Chief Executive Officer of Designed for Greatness, LLC, and Women of Destiny Empowerment Enterprises, Cheryl leverages her extensive experience and passion for personal development to inspire transformative growth in others.

Cheryl's literary journey began with the release of her first book, *In the Arms of Jesus: Favor, Increase and Promotion*, in 2019, followed by the impactful *Divine Keys to Unlocking Your Destiny*. Since then, she has authored five additional books, each contributing to her mission of empowering and inspiring others. In addition to her books, Cheryl has created a plethora of journals designed to guide readers in their personal and spiritual growth, offering practical tools for reflection and self-discovery.

Her love for writing dates back to her childhood, when she would spend countless hours crafting stories and poems. Recognizing the profound power of her words to effect positive change, Cheryl pursued writing with a fervent dedication that has only deepened over time. Her works are infused with themes of hope, resilience, and divine guidance, drawing from her personal experiences and her unwavering belief in the power of faith and divine timing.

Cheryl's life mission is to empower women to navigate life's trials with grace and purpose, ultimately leading them to a fulfilling and purposeful existence. Her personal experiences with adversity have fortified her belief in the power of divine intervention and the importance of trusting in God's perfect timing. These challenges have not only strengthened her resolve but have also enriched her writing, making her messages of hope and transformation deeply impactful.

In addition to her roles as a life coach and author, Cheryl is a dynamic speaker who engages audiences with her heartfelt messages and practical wisdom. Her seminars and workshops have transformed the lives of many, equipping them with the tools and insights needed to overcome obstacles and seize opportunities.

Cheryl is also actively involved in various philanthropic initiatives, supporting causes related to women's empowerment and community development. Her commitment to giving back reflects her belief in the collective power of individuals to create positive change.

With an unwavering dedication to unlocking human potential, Dr. Cheryl Dyson-Bennett continues to inspire and uplift individuals, helping them navigate their journeys with confidence and purpose. Her work stands as a testament to the transformative power of faith, resilience, and the pursuit of greatness.

CHERYL DYSON-BENNETT'S PUBLICATIONS

In the Arms of Jesus: Favor, Increase, and Promotion

Divine Keys to Unlocking Your Destiny: A 30-Day Journey to Unlocking Your Destiny

Divine Keys to Letting Go: A Guide to Mastering and Unleashing the Greatness in You, Let Go, and Take Charge of Your Life

Jesus Loves Me

Illuminating Your Path with God's Word: A 52-Guided Devotional to Enlighten Your Journey through Daily Prayers and Confessions

Journals

Pray, Trust, Wait, and Repeat

Divine Keys to Letting Go Prayer Journal

Anointed and Appointed Prayer Journal

I Am Blessed and Highly Favored Journal

Phenomenal Woman Prayer Journal

www.ingramcontent.com/pod-product-compliance
Lightning Source LLC
LaVergne TN
LVHW061556070526
838199LV00077B/7068